Edwin Arlington Robinson
and His Manuscripts

BY

ESTHER WILLARD BATES

WATERVILLE, MAINE

Colby College Library

1944

Edwin Arlington Robinson
and His Manuscripts

These brief informal meetings, for we all conscientiously returned to work at the end of an hour, opened the way to a mention of Robinson's need for someone to type his poetry, someone who could read his microscopic writing where n's and v's and r's were almost indistinguishable from one another. My myopic eyes were perfectly adapted to what William Vaughn Moody called his "immoral fist," and the copying began then and continued through his last long poem, *King Jasper*. I was not the only copyist. Three or four other friends and colonists took a turn occasionally. But most of it came to me.

My first Colony letter to my mother describes him: "Mr. Robinson is deaf, shy, and very unapproachable, and he never makes any advances conversationally to anyone. Conversations with him are largely questions on my part, pauses on his, and then the briefest possible response. Another question from me, another pause, another telegraphically brief reply, and so on."

But he soon talked, at least a little more, for my next letter says, "Mr. Robinson asked me for my butter at breakfast this morning. I told him I should tell my grandchildren I had provided the celebrated poet with butter. He said he had only asked for it, in order that I might. He also remarked the other day that Tennyson was a terrible ass, that the adulation of the British public was too much for him. This was apropos of the question, whether or not a

poet or composer could or should have an enor-
mous regard for himself or his work. Mr. Robinson
said he could never get up much enthusiasm either
for himself or his work."

Yet, one summer evening, walking up West Peterborough to see the deserted settlement, and the
dark silent mill with its velvet black water, he told
me he was, perhaps, two hundred years in advance
of his time, indicating in brief half-statements with
pauses in between, that his habit of understate-
ment, his absorption in the unconscious and semi-
conscious feelings and impulses of his characters
were the qualities in which he was unlike his con-
temporaries. He believed his work would live,
though he confessed to plenty of intermittent
doubtings. He said he wondered if he wasn't too
dry, too plain, if he wasn't overdoing the simple,
the unpoetic phrase. We looked a long time at the
brimming water above the dam. The poem be-
ginning

> *The miller's wife had waited long,*
> *The tea was cold, the fire was dead;*
> *And yet there might be nothing wrong*
> *In how he went and what he said*

was written about that same deserted mill.[2]

He seemed to my comparative youth a man considerably advanced into middle age — he was then
forty-four — so I asked him how it was that he had

[2] "The Mill" first appeared in the *New Republic*, July 2,
1919, and was collected in *The Three Taverns* in 1920.

published so little work,[3] and if he had been too much occupied by wage-earning of some sort. No, he said, he had never done much of anything except write, that in his youth he had had absolutely no sense of the passing of time. "Curious personality" another letter to my mother reads. "He comes over to my studio and sits as silent as a sphinx, but obviously comfortable. Then I relapse into silence, too. We eat our lunch. He smokes a couple of cigarettes. Promptly at two he leaves, pausing in the doorway to say that I may ask him again whenever I feel like it. I asked him the other day if he was never lonely. He said in his youth he was, but never now. Sometimes he wishes that he might be."

One of the early poems to be copied was "Rahel to Varnhagen." First he brought it over for me to read aloud to him, so he could see how it sounded. I did so, interrupted by muttered protests whenever I got a wrong inflection. Nevertheless, he entrusted me with the typing. He called the poem an interpretive monologue.[4] Rahel is opening her heart to Varnhagen, so much her junior, before she tells him at the end that she will marry him. A copy of Ellen Key's biography, *Rahel Varnhagen*, was in the bookcase just outside his Colony Hall bedroom, and he had picked it up, read it, and found it con-

---

[3] He had published three books of his poems: *The Children of the Night*, 1897; *Captain Craig*, 1902; and *The Town Down the River*, 1910.

[4] It was first published in *The Three Taverns*, 1920.

tained a good subject for a dramatic monologue. But he said he did not take his character from Ellen Key's book, nor did he draw directly from life in any of his poems. He said he "precipitated his own characters."

Lancelot, the first version, was the first long poem that I typed. It was declined by Macmillan, and a few years later was picked up by a new publisher, Thomas Seltzer, who was on the lookout for distinguished names. But before it was printed, *Merlin* was completed and also given me to type.[5] Because at that time I was still doubting my own accuracy in deciphering the pencilled script, I put marginal queries here and there, with only the intention of assuring absolute accuracy. The second and re-written version of *Lancelot* soon began to arrive by mail in sections of five or six hundred lines, and with them these comments:

"I find, in seeing the poem in the full flare of type, that I shall dispense with many of my experimental lines, and restore them, more or less, to the general metrical scheme of *Merlin*. I gather from your marginal comments that this will not displease you; and I fancy it will have the same effect on others. The long lines are all right, if read with the proper stress and speed, but I know well enough that I cannot count upon the attention and

[5] *Merlin* was published in 1917, but not until 1920 did Seltzer publish *Lancelot* in an edition of "450 copies for the Lyric Society."

indulgence that such reading will require. Hence the knife."

He writes again: "Thank you for the Transcript clipping. I am naturally grateful to W. S. B.[6] for all he says, though I wish for the most sordid of reasons that he wouldn't write such formidable long sentences, or find such world-shaking significance in the colors that Vivian put on to make Merlin take notice before she got tired of having him around.[7] She may have been speaking in sym-

[6] William Stanley Braithwaite, poetry editor of the *Boston Transcript*, and editor of the annual *Anthology of Magazine Verse*, in which poems by E. A. R. appeared in 1913, 1914, 1915, 1916, 1919, and 1923.

[7] "Are you always all in green, as you are now?"
    Said Merlin. . . .
    Said Vivian, leading Merlin with a laugh: . . .
    "And if I go in green, why, let me go so . . ."

    The lady Vivian in a fragile sheath
    Of crimson, dimmed and veiled ineffably
    By the flame-shaken gloom wherein she sat
    . . . heard Merlin coming.

On these lines Braithwaite remarked, in the *Transcript* for June 12, 1920: "Her entire garmenture . . . was prophetic . . . , the symbols clashing a sort of cloth-of-gold pageantry of ancient Britain, but the translation of these symbols [reveals] the foundation and fact of the shuddering and shocking catastrophe of the Great War . . . The modern world had gone on before our very gaze covering up the bones of its appalling purpose for war and disaster with every color of moral, political and economic deception until circumstance forged the arrival of the ripe hour for the loosening of the thunderbolt."

bols, but I had never thought of that particular speech as anything more than a little sassy."

Whether Seltzer had already accepted *Lancelot* when this letter was despatched, I do not recall, but E. A. R. continued to make revisions. In February, 1918, he writes: "I have shortened it by about five hundred lines, and tightened it up generally, with the result, I believe, that it goes along much more smoothly and tells itself with less fuss. I knew all along, down in my artistic gizzard, that I was going technically too far in the original version, although I wasn't quite ready to say so, even to myself."

One rainy day I ran through the wet Peterborough woods to Katharine Stetson's studio for some of her hot coffee, and found that E. A. R. had also dropped in. We pooled our luncheon supplies and ate together before her fire. "Mr. Robinson," I wrote my mother, "purred like a contented kitten and looked like an amused rabbit. He talked about Percy MacKaye, saying, a little enviously, that he had plenty of self-esteem and took himself and his work seriously every moment of his life, that he had a sense of fun but not a sense of humor. He said Ridgely Torrence had an abundance of both, and that he thought he would write something remarkable some day. . . . Mr. Robinson has a new play coming out, called *The Porcupine*."

There were several years in which E. A. hoped to see either this play or *Van Zorn* given a Broadway production.[8] As acting material, these plays still seem shadowy, and yet, if one or the other could be tried out, not by a merely competent company but with a cast and a director both having a rare sensitivity and subtlety, with a finely-wrought *mise-en-scène*, and played to an audience also attuned to delicate shadings and implications, it is possible that certain qualities might come to life and light that would explain the author's dogged faith in his own play-writing.

I failed to understand *Van Zorn* and wrote its author what was evidently a sad betrayal of my own ineptitude, for the following letter came swiftly back to me: "I'm sorry, too, that you, like so many others, have missed what I was driving at in the play. It was written for the stage — too much so, in fact — and I fear the stage will (or would) be absolutely necessary to make the thing intelligible. Van Zorn is supposed to believe that he 'found his destiny' in Villa Vannevar, but finds in Act II that he has been working unconsciously for Lucas, who is equally ignorant of what is going on. Villa knows by this time that Van Zorn is in love with her, and this fact, together with the realization that she is going to get Lucas after all, and through the un-

[8] *Van Zorn* was produced in 1917 by the Brooklyn Community Theatre Company at the building of the Young Men's Christian Association in that city and had a week's run, but neither of Robinson's plays ever appeared on Broadway. Macmillan published *Van Zorn* in 1914 and *The Porcupine* in 1915.

conscious sacrifice of a man who would probably have got her himself, if Lucas hadn't been in the way, shakes her up considerably. I suppose the trouble is that I tried to do too much. The play is for the most part the working of character upon character, the plot being left, more or less, to reveal itself by inference. If the thing has vitality enough to be 'cussed and discussed' sufficiently, people will come eventually to understand and accept it. Otherwise it will probably die an easy death, if not a sudden one. I made a misleading mistake, too, in calling it a comedy. So far as Van Zorn is concerned, it is a tragedy; and it is supposed to open or partly open all sorts of trap doors and windows that will give people glimpses into their own cellars and dooryards, and incidentally a fairly good view of the sun, moon and stars.

"In one sense it is more a poem than a play. In another sense, the good Lord only knows what it is, or what it is worth. In the light of my experience with other things of mine, I can only say that I don't believe that I could feel quite as I do about it, if there weren't something in it. But the only sensible thing for me to do now is to forget about it and work at other things — which will, in all probability, be about as intelligible as Van Zorn."

The playwright died hard in him. Once he said, "When I die, they ought to put D. D. — Defeated Dramatist — on my tombstone."

The magazine *Poetry* was having an anniversary

number and Harriet Monroe had written Robinson, asking for a contribution. He told me, somewhat obscurely, that he wanted some sort of a story with a "dead hand" theme, and wondered if my mother, whose mind was a storehouse of legends and traditions, knew one. My letter to her asks, "Do you know any true stories which have never been used in verse or drama or fiction about the dead hand? Metaphorically speaking. About some strong-willed person who inflicted his or her influence long after death on the surviving members of his family? Mr. Robinson is on the hunt for one, and wants to know if you have anything of the sort."

She didn't, and he made up his own. It was the poem in which the dead hand was the sister's love for her dead brother, and which keeps her from making what might have been a happy marriage. He wrote me, concerning it, "It is a great pity there aren't a few more ways in which we mortals may go wrong and make fools of ourselves generally. Perhaps you will say this again after reading my "Mortmain" poem. Harriet Monroe wished the name changed, thinking the original too ominous for a possibly dying magazine. Women again."

The last two words refer to a mild but continuous argument we had, in which I maintained he did not understand women, and he maintained they were illogical and contrarious. To please Miss Monroe he changed the name of "Mortmain" to

"Avenel Gray," but the change was for the magazine only. When it appeared in his next volume of
poetry, it was under its original title.[9]

Early in June, 1922, Mary Colum said at the
MacDowell Colony that Yale was going to give
Mr. Robinson an honorary degree; she said she
"got it through the air." Yale did, and one of my
family letters runs: "Mr. Robinson returned from
Yale, where he has just received a Litt.D., in as high
spirits as ever I saw him, mostly evinced by fre-
quent, brief, dry sallies and a light in his eyes. So
far, nobody has got any information out of him,
though he has been bombarded with questions.
. . . He confided to me that Harvard had asked him
to give the Phi Beta Kappa poem this year — this is
strictly confidential — but that he 'didn't have the
courage to do it,' saying that all the P B K poems
he had ever seen were so bad."

This was the year when Vachel Lindsay was
later asked to give it, and did.

"Yesterday he [E. A. R.] brought over to my
studio a letter from Macmillan, suggesting a four-
volume, pocket edition, in leather, of his collected
poems for the Christmas trade. Incidentally they
spoke of having sold five thousand copies of *Collected Poems*, and were now giving them another
printing. He wasn't exactly pleased with their pro-
posal, 1, because he thought they wouldn't succeed

[9] "Avenel Gray" appeared in *Poetry*, October, 1922.
"Mortmain" was collected in *Dionysus in Doubt* in 1925.

in selling them; 2, because he thought the small-sized page would necessitate slicing off the margins of the present-sized page (they will print from the same plates) and poetry absolutely needed wide margins; 3, Macmillan will not advertise the pocket edition enough, and 4, his new book, *Roman Bartholow*, would then be put off till spring, since it doesn't seem to be the thing for an author to get out two books at a time. . . .

"Later he said he thought he would take up with their offer, since he did not intend to get out another book for three years, and putting off *Roman Bartholow* until next spring would shorten the stretch.[10] He began talking about this new book, saying it was 4000 lines and he didn't believe anybody on earth would read it. He had been turning it over in his mind for eleven years. I asked him if he had it in for women as much in this book as in the others. This query sent him off into apologetic detours of thought, and finally he said he didn't think he had it in for women any more than the world had it in for women."

I had also protested against Lancelot's icy treatment of Guinevere in the sixth and seventh cantos, and his brusque

> "So, for a time, there will be no more war;
> And you are going back to Camelot"

[10] *Roman Bartholow* came out in 1923. It was followed the very next year by *The Man Who Died Twice*.

that sends her crashing floorward, and the even more heartless words of the following morning:

> . . . *"Well, are you well*
> *Again? Are you as well again as ever?"*

But the protest only made E. A. R. tighten up his mouth and say that Lancelot "had to."

Several months later, after *Roman Bartholow* was published and I had asked some trivial question about a phrase or two, he wrote: "It would be futile for me to pretend my work is always transparent. . . . If you and others can like half of what I do, you will be doing your share." This was one of only two occasions I can ever recall when he acknowledged that he might possibly be a little obscure. Usually when the charge was brought, he would say, "They don't read me!" — meaning, of course, read with care.

One letter to my mother about this time gives a sidelight on the mooted question of Robinson's pessimism. After describing how several of us were seated around one of the dining tables in a pleasant summer twilight, which darkened about us as we talked, I went on: "Very interesting conversation in the dark last night about pessimism. Mr. Robinson said he was a pessimist only in so far as this world was concerned, that he did not see how any thinking man could refuse to admit that there was more grief and suffering than anything else, but that he looked to other existences to answer the

problem. Fred Ballard asked what a father should
teach his child about the scheme of the world. Pad-
riac Colum said he should teach his boy that life
was a battle ground where he would fight a losing
fight, but he must be genial. "Fight, but be genial."
Mr. Robinson said, apropos of Hardy's pessimism,
that Hardy's blunder, both philosophic and artistic, was his reiteration of the idea of God jesting
with mankind. Henry Beston said that J. C. Squire
told him that if Hardy lived five more years, he'd
turn Christian after all, and then he quoted from
the ending of *The Dynasts:*

> *Last as first the question rings*
> *Of the Will's long travailings;*
> *Why the All-mover,*
> *Why the All-prover*
> *Ever urges on and measures out the chordless chime of Things.*

"Returning to pessimism, they talked of 'The
City of Dreadful Night' and Henry Beston said he
thought the sermon preached by the priest in that
poem to be the worst utterance of pessimism in all
literature."

Later on I hunted up and reread the poem, and
could not help agreeing. The urgent advice to
man, to end his life when he will, comes after the
bitter stanza:

> *And now at last authentic word I bring,*
> *Witnessed by every dead and living thing;*
> *Good tidings of great joy, for you, for all:*
> *There is no God; no Fiend with name divine*
> *Made us and tortures us; if we must pine,*
> *It is to satiate no Being's gall.*

The letter continues, "Robinson asked if anyone had ever read George Eliot's letter to Thomson, rebuking him for his melancholy, and Thomson's reply. He said it must have finished any attempt by George Eliot to continue the argument. Padraic Colum said the three great pessimists of the last century were Byron, Leopardi and Schopenhauer. Somebody said that all the world's greatest men were pessimists. Homer was; and Dante, surely. Was Shakespeare? And when they reckoned up his tragedies and the order in which he had written them, they concluded he was, too."

I had considerable curiosity about that exchange of letters which E. A. R. referred to, and after some hunting, located them in the *Life of James Thomson* by H. S. Salt. George Eliot's letter runs as follows:

I trust that an intellect informed by so much passionate energy as yours will soon give us more heroic strains with a wider embrace of human fellowship in them. . . . To accept life and write much fine poetry is to take a very large share in the quantum of human good, and seems to draw with it necessarily some recognition, affectionate and even joyful, of the manifold willing labours which have made such a lot possible.

Thomson apparently could not resist replying with a touch of bitter mimicry,

I have no Byronic quarrel with my fellows, whom I find all alike crushed under the iron yoke of Fate, and few of whom I can deem worse than myself, while so many are far better, and I certainly have an affectionate and even joyful recognition of the willing labours of those who have striven to alleviate our lot, though I cannot see that all their efforts have availed much against the primal curse of our existence. Has the world been the better or the worse for the life of even such a man as Jesus? I cannot judge; but I fear on the whole considerably the worse.

An undated note to my mother, probably written during the summer of 1922, says that E. A. R.'s "new book is not yet finished, but may be out in the fall. He said his short poems were ready in his mind; yet, though he has several in the oven, he wasn't going to take them out till they were well-baked. He said he took out the sonnet "Job the Rejected" before it was done, and it never pleased him.[11] Apropos of the Pulitzer Prize, he said he thought all these prizes carried a sort of a stigma, though they weren't as bad as prize contests. This was the prize awarded him for his *Collected Poems*. A few days later he spoke again of his strictures on the Pulitzer awards, saying he did not mean really to condemn them.

"He said"— this is later on, but in the same letter —"John Drinkwater wrote him, apropos of his article on Mr. Robinson in the *Yale Review*, apologizing for his [Drinkwater's] vagueness, saying that England being in her present state of mind, he didn't dare to state his admiration for Mr. Robinson's poetry as strongly as he would have other-

[11] This poem first appeared in the New York Evening Post's *Literary Review*, January 22, 1921.

wise. The same review has appeared simultane-
ously in some English periodical."[12]

This "present state of mind" was probably the
feeling of resentment in England over our comments on her non-payment of the so-called "war
debt," and brings to mind an anecdote that Robinson ruefully told after his return from London. He
borrowed a small sum from someone on the train,
and then found he didn't have the right change to
repay it. The Englishman said, "Oh, never mind.
Put it on the debt." E. A. confessed to feeling a
little disconcerted.

Almost every time a manuscript came to be
copied, a note of slight apology, a phrase or two of
doubt, accompanied it. Typical are the remarks
about *The Glory of the Nightingales*. For instance,
in mid-July he writes: "My new poem is written
on a new plan,— the first 800 lines being mostly
preparation. If it proves to be dull, as it may, I shall
cut unmercifully and shall ask you to be equally
unmerciful when you read it. You will please read
it as if it were by an unknown minstrel. . . . . If
the long preamble isn't interesting enough to hold
the attention for what is coming, it would be fatal
to print it." The next letter, a few weeks later, says,
"Today I have finished the first draft of the second

[12] It appeared in the *Fortnightly Review*, London, April
1, 1922, and was reprinted in the London edition of Robinson's *Collected Poems*, published in 1922.

half of *Nightingale*, and hope to have it copied and
more or less rewritten in about three weeks, when
I shall be going to Boston. I hope you will find
Nightingale a not altogether negligible person, although he wasn't, or isn't, in all ways a model citi-
zen. Somehow model citizens don't make good
poems. . . . It is asking an awful lot of anybody to
read a long poem, and I'm still subject to surprise
when told that one of mine has been read, and even
read twice. That's about the only thing left that
does surprise me."

Another note said: "Dr. Malory goes to Sharon
by a route that is shorter by some 200 lines. He
goes much better."

He acknowledges the typed copy: "I am glad
to have *Nightingale* in your typewritten copy and
I'm greatly obliged to you for making him look
so well. I hope you are rather right in your general
approval of him. The poem as a whole seems to
me rather good, and I should fancy that a considerable number of people might like it. It is full of sun-
shine and ends happily—with only one suicide—
and should make those who read it feel warm and
pleasant all over."

Robinson seemed to be in unusually high spirits
when he was writing *Tristram*, and moved about
with an air of quiet elation, as an author is apt to
do when his work is going well. I seem to recall
that he wore the same general air of pleasurable ex-
citement when he was writing *Lancelot*. Incident-

ally this poem was called *Lancelot and Guinevere* all through its writing and until the copying of the second version. *Tristram* also was *Tristram and Isolt* until it was ready for the printer. Once while talking about this latter poem, he said he had been considering his work as a whole, and realized that he had never written anything which treated of love as a complete and powerful theme in itself. (These are not his exact words but only my recollection of them.) So, to remedy this lack, he turned to the Tristram story. The Wagnerian opera had long been a special favorite with him. Another time he said, "You know this sort of thing happens every day," and to my look of inquiry he added, "I mean people love the way Tristram and Isolt were supposed to . . . It is not rare . . . It happens."

He gave me the script to copy, canto by canto, with amusing commentary. It bothered him to find the right epithets. "I am still in doubt as to some of the mushy parts, but I don't suppose that Isolt would call Tristram 'Dear Sir,' or that he would call her 'Dear Madam.' But I'll let it stand for the present. Now I'm set to go over the whole 4400 lines and see what I find. If it looks long to me, how is it going to look to others? I'm glad I don't know."

In another note, and along the same idea, he added, "Sentimentality is far worse than death." When I praised Morgan Le Fay's letter in *Tristram*, he admitted it was a good letter, saying whimsically, "I wish I could write as good a one myself."

The ruthless cutting he often gave his early drafts almost always aroused a protest from me, for lines went into the wastebasket that were often rich in beauty or wisdom. One protest he replied to thus: "The lines you like are well enough as lines, but the passage seems to me now rather out of place, and about the last thing that Isolt would have said. I remember that my subconscious watchdog (who isn't always on his job) growled a little while I was writing them. The Lancelot part that bothers you comes in a passage of about 300 lines that I threw away last winter.[18] The thing was getting so long that it scared me." The discarded lines were

When we are gone, tales everywhere of us
Will have an end we shall not hear.

A letter from him in November, 1931, says: "I am greatly pleased to know that you find peace in my work. Some people call it gloom, which of course it isn't." Another note touches on the same subject — his alleged pessimism: "What you say of *Talifer* cheers me up. About this time of year I always have a critical slump and feel my summer has been lost. But it is much too late to do much about it. Most of the poetic fellows have curled up before coming to my age — excepting the Greek tragedians, who kept themselves healthy and hap-

[18] The "Lancelot part" was where the knight let the lovers, Tristram and Isolt, stay at Joyous Gard.

py by writing about nothing but murder and worse. Maybe I've been too cheerful."

And regarding *Amaranth:* "Thank you for all the good things you say about *Amaranth* . . . I like it myself, but there is a possibility of my being slightly prejudiced. From present indications *Talifer* isn't going to fare very well in the newspapers, and will have to go mainly on its own feet.

"The critics, except Ranck[14] and Untermeyer, didn't seem to understand that it is a comedy. It is always dangerous to be different. The Lord only knows what they will make of the new poem [*Amaranth*]."

He was disappointed that *Talifer* was not instantly recognized as the light-hearted piece of irony that he meant it to be. During the years when he was writing the longer poems, the ones that included *The Glory of the Nightingales* and *The Man Who Died Twice,* he would say something as follows: "Well, So-and-so [naming the most recent of them] seem to be going. If people like that sort of thing, I can go on doing it." He was not implying that they were pot-boilers, but simply he found he had unearthed some more of his peculiar metal from a deep and not-likely-to-be-exhausted lode. It is a pity that more people do not read them, not only for their poetry, but for their

[14] Edwin Carty Ranck, newspaperman and critic, was long one of E. A. R.'s most valued friends.

shrewd, astute, inimitable human commentary.

Once, during his later years, he said sadly, "People ask me why I do not do the short poems any more. I can't. They don't come any more. At least, not good ones. And I'm not willing to publish poems I know are inferior to the early ones." He was silent for a few moments. Then he said again, "They don't come any more."

Usually he spoke of his work with a half-humorous, half-apologetic air. Yet if someone praised it discriminatingly, he would admit judicially that it had some value. When I first saw the sonnet "Many Are Called,"[15] and exclaimed over it, he said, "Yes, that's a poem. You could call that a poem." Then he explained that some of his other sonnets were written for their idea, or because they held up some fragment of humanity for a moment's contemplation, or because they turned a light on some aspect of life, adding that he realized they did not have so much in the way of poetic beauty as the lines which begin

> *The Lord Apollo, who has never died,*
> *Still holds alone his immemorial reign.*

This occasion was the only other time when he admitted obscurity, and he then had reference to the sonnets, "Modernities," "Ben Trovato," and "The Tree in Pamela's Garden." These and a few others he would demand that I elucidate to him,

[15] It was first printed in *The New Republic*, November 3, 1920.

but he would never wholly admit that I had read their riddles exactly.[16]

To one carefree, young inquisitor at the Colony, who asked him if he wrote free verse, he replied dryly, no, that he wrote badly enough, as it was.

He had a special liking for his "Rembrandt to Rembrandt," saying that next to "The Man Against the Sky" he thought it might be, perhaps, the best thing he ever did.[17] He liked his "Nicodemus" and was greatly pleased to have it praised by certain friends whose judgment he trusted. Padraic Colum was one of these. He said he had always liked the sonnet, "A Song at Shannon's," ever since he wrote it.[18] He felt that "Two Gardens in Linndale" deserved a place in anthologies as much as the inevitable "Miniver Cheevy." "Two Gardens" has always seemed as though it must be autobiographic.[19] He liked "On The Way," the dialogue in blank verse between Alexander Hamilton and Aaron Burr, and had been moved to write it after reading F. S. Oliver's *Alexander Hamilton: an Essay on American Union.* The late Henry Cabot Lodge

[16] "The Tree in Pamela's Garden" first appeared in *The New Republic,* November 24, 1920; "Ben Trovato," in *The Nation,* January 26, 1921; and "Modernities," in *The Dial,* May, 1921.

[17] First printed in *Collected Poems,* 1921.

[18] It first appeared in *The Lyric,* New York, March, 1919, and was collected in *The Three Taverns* in 1920.

[19] First published in *The Town Down the River,* 1910.

sent him a letter praising this poem, and E. A. R. brought it round to my studio to show it to me, adding characteristically, "Please don't mention this to anyone."

E. A. R. would talk about whatever he was writing, either before he got to work on it, or while it was under way, with a kind of wide vague allusiveness which gave almost no clue as to what it was really going to be. He spoke again and again of *Amaranth* as a kind of dream poem. . . . "No, not a dream poem . . . well, a kind of . . . (pause) well, I don't know what you'll make of it." Or regarding *King Jasper:* "Do you know what an allegory is? Well, I'm writing an allegory. No, not an allegory. Well, it might be called an allegory. I don't know. (pause) Yes, as much as anything, it is an allegory. But I don't know what you'll make of it."

As to his methods of work, of course he had habits, and of course he varied them. Once he remarked that he had a system of his own when it came to the long poems. He had their sequence of events all planned before he came to the MacDowell Colony on June first, all worked out, "as you do the scenario to a play," he said. Then when he arrived at Peterborough the actual writing began. Over a period of some years the four summer months saw one of these long poems begun, and a first draft completed. This he would give me to copy, and before he left Boston in December, where he had a brief way-station, as it were, on

West Newton Street, I would send him the type-
script. He would not look at it then. He would let
it rest until he reached New York, and then he
would go over it and revise it, not making any extensive changes. A few revised pages would come
back to me for re-copying. Then a few minor
emendations and the manuscript would go to the
printer.

At Peterborough he was slow in getting under
way, he told some of us. Although he sat faithfully
down at his studio table by nine o'clock each morn-
in, he did not often actually get much down on
paper till about eleven or thereabouts. At one, he
stopped and ate his Spartan lunch of crackers and
milk and drank some strong black tea. Then, he
rested a little, and after that walked back to Colony
Hall, sometimes with letters, always carrying his
lunch basket. Half an hour later he wandered
slowly back to his studio through the beautiful
hemlock woods and resumed writing. Frequently
he found the late afternoon hours between four
and six the most productive of the entire day. Perhaps it was this leisurely waiting for the mood and
for the words which made him put down his final
phrasing so often in his first drafts.

If, when he first arrived at the Colony, several
days passed before his work got well launched, he
was genuinely distressed. If more days of fruitless
waiting occurred, he would say he must leave the
place. But sooner or later the tidal wave rolled in,

and the work, once begun, usually moved uninter-
ruptedly along until it was completed, leaving him
feeling, he said, "like a weary woodchuck."

The manuscripts which came to me were always
in pencil, beautifully, if microscopically, written.
Punctuation was always flawless, but a minor mistake in spelling might creep in, perhaps once in ten
to twenty pages. The poem's very first draft was
rarely given to me. I would see him stow it away
in the drawer of the little corner table in the Veltin
Studio. He had made his own clear copy from this.
Once in a while I had a look at a first draft of some
poem. There were rarely very extensive revisions,
and I never saw a page as lined and under-lined
with corrections as, for instance Keats' *St. Agnes*,
or Byron's *Don Juan*. Typical corrections were
cuttings of from two to twenty lines, and the
slight alterations necessary to make the lopped
lines connect properly. Now and then he substi-
tuted a more apt or more poetic or more unusual
word or phrase. In such lyrics as I saw, four to
eight of the opening lines remained exactly as written, and later ones — those that followed — were
revised and polished. Apparently his rhyming was
often beautifully spontaneous, and I never hap-
pened to see corrections that looked as if he were
on the hunt for rhymes. They rather looked as if
he were working for subtlety or exactitude.

When he finished copying a page from his first
draft, he always drew a long slanting pencilled line

down the entire length of the original page, as if to indicate a sense of pleased accomplishment at having made progress. Lines to be added or inserted were written along the wide margin of his pages, in fine beautiful regular parallels, perfectly spaced, and then their placing accurately indicated with an encircling line and arrow.

As with all other writers, he wanted to know how his work struck its first reader, and it was not always easy to make an adequate and satisfying response at the drop of the hat. He was sensitive to an unbelievable degree. One had to be very careful not to say anything which could be interpreted or misinterpreted as critical or in the slightest way unfavorable. His reaction was imperceptible at first, but any wound buried itself in his heart and mind and endured. It did not rankle exactly, but it did live on. Unimportant and ignorant people seemed to have as much power to hurt or dismay as any other kind. He was defenceless, so far as his feeling about his poetry went, but he could defend himself from other kinds of rudeness, or utter a rebuke with a devastating icy brevity.

Habitually, in conversation, he made oblique statements, or under-statements, or statements of implication, only. Because of a deep-seated caution and an equally deep reserve, he disliked being required to be explicit. Sometimes these qualities made hard going in daily converse. Not uncommonly they led to minor misunderstandings, and those he preferred, it sometimes seemed, to leave unravelled. As in his poetry, it was as if he liked to leave the enigma undisturbed, when brought face to face with it. Something was lost in the process of elucidation.

He liked to have the other person talk to him, so he could agree, or, more frequently and more emphatically, disagree. He liked shop talk and talk about creative processes in general. Once we were talking about the mystery of the imagination. One could walk across a room on a certain day, at a certain hour and minute, I said, and one's sequence of thought be altered without warning or will, by something one sees or hears, in the room or out of the window, or by a movement or something caught through any of the senses. Threads of thought cross each other and take fire, and to a writer's surprise and delight something kindles which may become his preoccupation for months and years. Yet, if he had not walked across that room idly, a certain dream and its fulfilment would never have possessed him.

"Yes," he said, "I've often thought of that, too."

Contrary to a statement sometimes made, E. A. R. both liked and trusted woman. He was the kindest and most loyal of friends to several women in the course of his life. It did not always seem, however, that he really had a very complete understanding of them. He had a fixed conviction of woman's inhumanity to woman. The feline instinct, he felt,

was invariably present, and he was generally look-
ing for it. He suspected nearly all women of guile,
innocent guile to be sure, but guile. He thought
they all had sharp tongues, whether or not they
were in use at the moment. I quoted to him once,
in appreciation, the lines from "Annandale
Again":[20]

> *She gratifies*
> *A casual need for giving pain;*
> *And having drawn a little blood,*
> *She folds her paws and purrs again.*

"Well," he nodded, "you do, you know. You
do!"

Someone asked him once about the place of
women as writers, compared with that of men. He
said thoughtfully that women were best, both as
writers and artists, when they wrote or painted as
women. When their work was most feminine, they
reached their heights, and he cited Mrs. Brown-
ing's sonnets and Jane Austen's novels.

He was a wide reader, a careful reader, and had
a long and exact memory. He quoted frequently
and always accurately. He knew his Bible.[21] One
lay on his writing table in the Veltin Studio, beside
the dictionary which he read literally and advised

[20] First printed in *Scribner's Magazine*, August 1929; collected in *Nicodemus*, 1932.

[21] Robinson's copy of The Oxford Self-Pronouncing
Bible, inscribed "E. A. Robinson" on the fly-leaf, is now in
the Colby College Library.

me to read.[22] Now and then he would show me a rare word he had found, and would use it humorously.

During the years in which he was engaged on the longer poems, especially *Cavender's House* and *Matthias at the Door*, I saw a volume or two of Ibsen's plays lying on his studio table. A volume of Milton was there more regularly; he said he liked to read Milton's blank verse when he was writing it himself.[23] When he was starting *Tristram*, he was reading Shakespeare's *Antony and Cleopatra*. He was amazingly familiar with English poetry, especially that of the nineteenth century. He knew Swinburne's plays enough to discuss and compare them. If I ran across, in my browsings, a less well-known poem, such as Robert Buchanan's *Book of Orm*, and would mention it, he would say quickly, "How do *you* come to be reading the *Book of*

[22] Robinson's copy of Webster's American Dictionary of the English Language, Springfield, Merriam, 1863, is now in the Colby College Library.

[23] Robinson's "volume of Milton" was The Globe Edition, London, Macmillan, 1887. It is now in the Colby College Library. The book is inscribed: "E. A. Robinson from L. J. H.," i.e., Lawrence J. Henderson, whom Robinson had met in Gardiner. Henderson later became Professor of Biology at Harvard. Robinson had previously owned the *Poetical Works of John Milton*, 2 vols., New York, John B. Alden, 1885, and had autographed them: "E. A. Robinson, May 27, 1887. G. H. S." (i.e., Gardiner High School). On April 17, 1893, he presented these volumes to his Harvard classmate, James L. Tryon. They are now in the Colby College Library.

Orm?" And he was sure to have read it himself. Dickens he knew by heart.[24]

Hardy he knew thoroughly and always admired, though his esteem rose at times, and at times diminished slightly. He felt a sound knowledge of him was essential to a fellow writer, and at varying times sent me odd volumes of the handy little red leather edition of Hardy's novels until the set was complete. There was never any lessening of his high opinion of *The Dynasts*. This, too, he gave me, adjuring me solemnly to read it carefully, but a little at a time.

Meredith he had apparently read with close attention, and compared novel with novel, especially liking *Richard Feverel* and *One of Our Conquerors*. "You women," he said, "ought to be grateful to Meredith. See what he does for you!"

One summer he was re-reading *Wuthering Heights* and urging the rest of us to read it again, saying it was an amazing book. He paid due regard to Virginia Woolf, but after he had finished reading *To the Lighthouse* with the attentiveness that book demanded, he said with a little smile he was glad when he "got there."

[24] In Robinson's boyhood home was The People's Edition of Charles Dickens' Complete Works, Boston, Estes & Lauriat, 1882, 15 vols. These books are now in the Colby College Library; each is autographed on the title-page "Edward Robinson," the poet's father. Also in the Colby Library is a copy of *Charles Dickens: A Critical Study*, by G. K. Chesterton, New York, Dodd Mead & Co., 1907, purchased by Robinson in 1908.

In regard to his own work he had the great man's inner assurance of its worth, balanced by the sensitive man's vulnerableness to attack and to temporary neglect. But I heard him make one statement in his early years, his middle years and his last years. It was that the life he lived was the only life possible for him, and that he wrote in the only way he could. "It's all I could have done, write poetry. I can't do anything else; I never could. And I have to write the kind of stuff I do write."

He spoke as though blind destiny led him, and not an inner dedication. It is for the rest of us to recognize the high awareness, the fastidious taste, the undeviating purpose of the poetic genius which has so enriched our century.

COLBY COLLEGE MONOGRAPH No. 11

This essay was first delivered as an address to the
Colby Library Associates in Waterville, Maine,
on Friday, October 15, 1943.

COLOPHON: TWO HUNDRED AND FIFTY COPIES
OF THIS BOOK HAVE BEEN PRINTED FOR THE
LIBRARY OF COLBY COLLEGE, IN WATERVILLE,
BY THE SOUTHWORTH-ANTHOENSEN PRESS IN THE
YEAR NINETEEN HUNDRED AND FORTY-FOUR.